I. The Growth Debate

During the 1980s and 1990s, European economies went through a period of slowing economic growth and high unemployment, a condition some economists described as "secular stagnation" or "secular decline." Across the major European economies, especially in Germany and France, economic growth hovered around 2 percent per year during that period, with unemployment ranging between 7 and 11 percent between 1982 and 2005, much in contrast to the robust growth and low unemployment those countries enjoyed during the early post-war decades. Economists pointed to generous welfare policies, government spending and inflexible labor markets as causes of slowing economic growth across the region. On the other side of the Atlantic, the United States enjoyed a robust recovery during those years by reducing taxes, eliminating regulations on business

The question today, after two decades of subpar growth, is whether or not the American economy has entered into its own era of secular decline.

curbing welfare spending and tightening monetary policy to control inflation and strengthen the dollar. The United States seemed to have a prescription for economic growth that either did not work or could not be tried in Europe.

The question today, after two decades of subpar growth, is whether or not the American economy has entered into its own era of secular decline. For five decades, from 1950 to 2000, the U.S. economy grew (on average) by 3 or 4 percent per year (in inflation-adjusted terms), such that Americans came to assume that robust growth, interrupted by recessions here and there, would continue steadily into the future. Yet over the past two decades the

U.S. economy has grown by just 2 percent per year on average, or about half the rate as in the 1950s and 1960s. Now some economists are beginning to wonder if this is the "new normal" for the American economy.

Former Treasury Secretary Lawrence Summers has drawn such a conclusion in a series of lectures and articles over the past several years, including his column for the *Vox* e-book *Secular Stagnation: Facts, Causes and Cures*. Summers pointed to lackluster growth and productivity since the year 2000, despite declining interest rates and exploding government debt. In the past, those conditions should have fueled more robust growth than has been the case over the past two decades. He used the term "secular stagnation" to describe the new situation, reviving a concept introduced in the 1930s by Keynesian economist Alvin Hansen to describe the disappointing recovery from the Great Depression. Summers suggested that economists and policy makers need new models and tools to deal with these new conditions.

Robert Gordon, in *The Rise and Fall of American Growth* (2016), documented that argument with historical data stretching back into the 19th century. Gordon concluded that the unprecedented economic growth Americans enjoyed during much of the 20th century was a singular event driven by an interconnected series of innovations unlikely to be repeated. The computer and the internet, along with their many contemporary applications, will not come close to matching the prosperity created a century ago by the development of electricity, the internal combustion engine, indoor plumbing and modern communications. Americans, he suggested, much like Europeans (and Japanese) should accommodate themselves to the new reality of slowing growth and slowly improving living standards.

Many reject that argument for a mix of psychological and technological reasons. Some say the secular stagnation thesis is far too pessimistic for Americans used to looking forward to an ever-improving future. Others suggest that the computer and the internet, along with cloud-based applications, will ignite a technological revolution that will promote economic growth and rising living standards in the decades ahead. These technologies, they point out, have already revolutionized important aspects of American life, and they will soon spread to new areas. These innovations show promise of restoring economic growth to the robust levels of the 1950s and 1960s. That may be so, but there is scant evidence of it thus far.

It is true that the U.S. economy grew by 5.7 percent in 2021, the largest annual gain since the 1980s, with an addition of some 6.1 million new jobs during the year. But those gains were mostly in the form of bouncebacks from unprecedented losses in 2020 due to the coronavirus pandemic when the economy contracted by 3.4 percent and some 9 million jobs disappeared. When the GDP rates from those two years are combined and averaged, the annual growth rate over these two years comes in at just over 2 percent, very close to the 2.3 percent rate in 2019 before the coronavirus lockdowns began. The growth in jobs was also mostly in the form of recovery from the job losses in 2020. Nor does it appear that the robust growth of 2021 will be sustained, since the Labor Department reported recently that the economy contracted by 1.6 percent in the first quarter of 2022 and by 0.9 percent in the second quarter. This – two consecutive quarters of contraction – meets the technical definition of a recession. In any case, there are few signs in the data that the U.S. economy is about to break out of its multi-decade slump.

The eventual outcome of this debate will matter a great deal to Americans in future decades. The difference between 4 percent and 2 percent annual growth, or the difference between levels of growth in the 1960s and the 2010s, approaches $500 billion in 2021 with a current GDP of $23 trillion, not to mention compounded annual shortfalls far into the future. This is America's "growth deficit," and it poses many challenges for a country accustomed to steady economic growth. Can the United States manage its exploding debt in the face of stagnating growth or, for that matter, the expensive promises to seniors in the form of Social Security and Medicare programs, not to mention pledges to other groups strewn throughout the federal budget? Can the United States sustain an $800 billion per year defense budget, along with its status as a world superpower on the foundation of a stagnating economy? Can an already polarized polity continue to function in an orderly manner with another decade or two of slow economic growth?

The answers to these questions, and many more like them, are "probably not." Much therefore depends upon a revival of the kind of economic growth the United States enjoyed during the half century from 1950 to 2000. That kind of revival is possible (few predicted the surge in post-war economic growth), but it is nowhere apparent in the growth rates of the past few decades.

The presentation below is based upon trends in economic growth, productivity, innovation, population and debt, with consideration of a few additional factors that may be impeding or encouraging economic growth, including the COVID-19 crisis of the past few years. Those trends point (tentatively) to continuing headwinds for the American economy and to further evidence for the stagnation thesis.

II. Economic Growth in the United States

Most Americans are aware that economic growth has slowed in recent years, though they may not know that this now looks like a long-term trend that goes back a half century or more. Economic growth in the United States peaked in the 1950s and 1960s, and it has gradually slowed, decade by decade, down to the present. This trend has been obscured by a few important factors, such as continuing low unemployment rates, declining inflation, historically low interest rates and a long boom in stock and bond markets.

Real Gross Domestic Product – GDP adjusted for inflation – accelerated during the 1950s and 1960s at impressive rates of between 4.0 and 4.5 percent per year, provoking descriptions of the "affluent society" and shaping extravagant expectations about future prospects regarding growth, consumption and leisure. President Lyndon Johnson could not

Much therefore depends upon a revival of the kind of economic growth the United States enjoyed during the half century from 1950 to 2000.

have passed his expensive Great Society agenda absent the robust economic growth of that era. In designing those programs, policy-makers assumed that the prosperity of that era would continue into the indefinite future. Johnson, along with many economists at the time, spoke as if the problem of growth had been solved. The challenge for government was to deploy accumulating wealth to improve the public's quality of life through expenditures on education, the arts and the environment. As Johnson declared in 1964 in his "Great Society" speech at the University of Michigan: "For half a century we called upon unbounded invention and untiring industry to create an order of plenty for all of our people. The challenge of the next half century is whether we have the wisdom to use that wealth to enrich and elevate our national life, and to advance the quality of our American civilization."

Yet, due to many factors, economic growth gradually slowed to an average of 3.3 percent per year in the 1970s amid unprecedented rates of inflation, rising gasoline prices, the collapse of the gold standard and a sequence of failed presidential administrations. Given the difficulties of that decade, such a rate of economic growth looks impressive in view of what happened in subsequent decades. Economic growth then fell slightly to an (average) annual rate of 3.1 percent in the 1980s, and to 3.2 percent in the 1990s, both successful decades in terms of economic performance and popular approval.

Economic growth then slowed to 1.9 percent from 2000 to 2009, thanks in part to the deep recession and financial crisis of 2008, and to 2.2 percent from 2010 to 2019 as the economy gradually recovered from the crisis. This slowdown proceeded under both Republican and Democratic presidents with different tax and spending policies. There was a small uptick in growth under President Trump between 2017 and 2019 prior to the coronavirus pandemic, but it was not large enough to disturb the overall trend.

A growth rate of around 2 percent per year appears to be the "new normal" today, compared to those 4 percent annual rates in the 1950s and 1960s and more than 3 percent during the 1980s and 1990s. Aside from 2021, when economic growth was inflated by recovery from the pandemic lockdowns, the U.S. economy has not grown by 5 percent per year since the 1980s, nor by 4 percent per year since the 1990s. If the economy had continued to grow over the decades at those earlier rates, then real GDP in 2022 would be more than double its current level. Lackluster growth goes a long way to explain several conditions, including income inequality, stagnant wages and salaries for American workers and perhaps even the sour mood of the American electorate in recent years.

This trend is illustrated in the chart below, which depicts percentage changes in annual GDP from 1950 to 2021 in the form of five-year moving averages (which smooths out annual changes to give a clearer picture of the long-term trend). The chart depicts a gradually descending slope of change in GDP decade by decade, with peaks in the mid-1950s and mid-1960s, followed by more modest peaks in the 1980s and 1990s, then a sharp

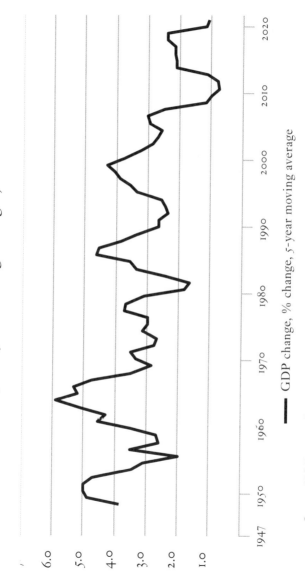

Figure 1: Year-to-Year Changes in U.S. GDP, 1948–2021
(Five-year moving averages)

— GDP change, % change, 5-year moving average

Source: U.S. Bureau of Economic Analysis, Real Gross Domestic Product [gdpC1], retrieved from
FRED, Federal Reserve Bank of St. Louis; https://fred.stlouisfed.org/series/gdpC1, July 26, 2022.

downward pattern from the early 2000s to the present. The troughs in the chart depict either recessions or longer periods of sluggish growth, as in the 1970s or recent decades.

The same trend appears when economic growth is measured in terms of real GDP per capita, which takes into account changes in population over the period. (That figure today – in 2012 dollars – is around $59,000 per year.) The chart below, again portrayed in terms of five-year moving averages, reveals a peak of nearly 6 percent growth in per capita income in the mid-1960s, with descending peaks in the mid-1980s at 3.5 percent and mid-1990s at just over 3 percent.

These latter peaks occurred during the Reagan and Clinton presidencies, which partly explains the popularity of those two presidents, both of whom stressed economic growth as a national priority. The steady downward trend gained speed after the year 2000 with weak recoveries from the recessions of 2001 and 2008–09. Prior to the coro-

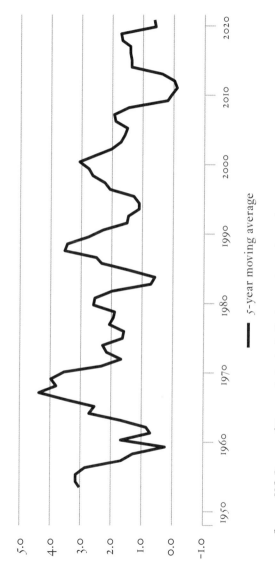

Figure 2: Year-to-Year Changes in Per Capita GDP, 1948–2021 (Five-year moving averages)

— 5-year moving average

Source: U.S. Bureau of Economic Analysis, Real gross domestic product per capita, retrieved from FRED, Federal Reserve Bank of St. Louis; https://fred.stlouisfed.org/series/A939RX0Q048SBEA, July 26, 2022.

navirus pandemic, per capita income growth was running at just 1 or 2 percent per year, or roughly half the rate of the period from 1960 to 2000.

No matter if economic growth is measured in terms of overall growth or per capita income, the figures clearly point to a steady downward trajectory from the late 1990s to the present.

III. Labor Force Expansion

Economic growth is generally a function of two factors: the number of workers and productivity per worker. A rapidly expanding workforce combined with increases in productivity lead to robust economic growth, as was the case in the United States in the 1950s and 1960s. As the workforce expands more slowly, or as productivity slows, the overall economy will contract or expand more slowly as well.

The Bureau of Labor Statistics has reported monthly since 1948 on the size of the civilian

> *Economic growth in the United States peaked in the 1950s and 1960s, and it has gradually slowed, decade by decade, down to the present.*

labor force in the United States. This is a comprehensive measure of the labor force that includes all people over the age of 16 who are either employed or seeking employment. The measure captures 80 percent of the workforce that contributes to GDP, though it excludes farm employees, proprietors and many self-employed workers, nor does it capture those potential workers who have given up on employment or who have otherwise dropped out of the workforce. But it is a consistent and reliable measure, used by the federal government to measure employment and un-employment, and by private sector analysts and forecasters who monitor changes in the labor force.

The civilian labor force grew at uneven rates from 61.6 million in 1950 to the current level of 164 million in 2022. The chart below depicts the percentage change in the labor force per year, portrayed again in terms of five-year moving averages.

As the chart shows, the size of the workforce expanded by increasing rates during the 1950s and 1960s at a time when the baby-boom generation was growing up and coming of age, but not yet fully in the labor force. During the 1950s, the workforce expanded at an average rate of 1.1 percent per year, with between 600,000 and 1,000,000 workers added per year. That rate accelerated during the 1960s as the workforce expanded during that decade at an average rate of 1.7 percent per year, with an addition of some 13 million new workers during the decade, a nearly 20 percent increase during the decade. The annual expansion of the workforce peaked during the 1970s with an average gain of 2.7

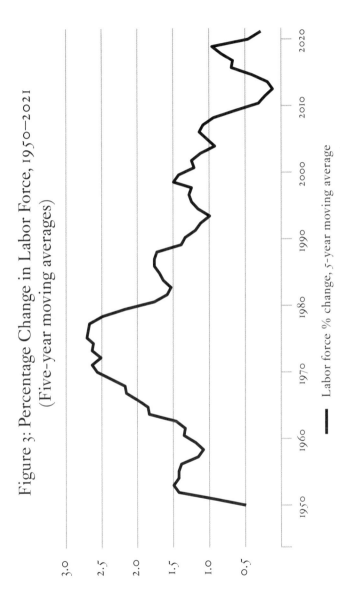

Figure 3: Percentage Change in Labor Force, 1950–2021
(Five-year moving averages)

— Labor force % change, 5-year moving average

Source: U.S. Bureau of Labor Statistics, Civilian Labor Force Level [CLF16OV], retrieved from
FRED, Federal Reserve Bank of St. Louis; https://fred.stlouisfed.org/series/CLF16OV, July 26, 2022.

percent per year as the baby-boom generation entered the workforce, with substantial increases in female workers adding to the overall totals. During that decade the labor force expanded by more than 24 million workers, or nearly 30 percent. In retrospect, the overall economy, with double-digit inflation and a serious recession in 1974–75, would not have performed nearly as well as it did without the addition of those new workers.

The labor force expanded at a lesser rate during the next two decades, by an average of 1.8 percent per year in the 1980s and 1.3 percent per year in the 1990s, due to lower birth rates from the late 1960s through the 1970s. All told, the workforce grew by 18 million from 1980 to 1989 and by nearly 16 million from 1990 to 1999. At that point, expansion of the labor force fell sharply to an average of 0.9 percent per year from 2000 to 2009, or by 13 million new workers during the decade, and 0.6 percent per year from 2010 to 2019, or 11.3 million new workers.

Over the past two decades the workforce

expanded by less than half the rate of the 1980s, and by less than a third of the rate during the 1970s. The U.S. economy added twice as many workers during the 1970s as it did during each of the two decades of the new century. It should come as no surprise, then, that the economy grew almost twice as fast during

---

A growth rate of around 2 percent per year appears to be the "new normal" today, compared to those 4 percent annual rates in the 1950s and 1960s and more than 3 percent during the 1980s and 1990s.

---

that decade as it did in the two most recent decades. This slowing in the expansion of the workforce is one large factor behind the gradual slowdown in recent decades in the overall economy.

The Labor Force Participation Rate (the percentage of the labor force working or seeking work) has also been declining in recent decades, thereby adding to the challenge of slowing population growth. The chart below depicts a rising participation rate from 59 percent in 1965 to 67 percent in the late 1990s, as the baby-boom generation and more women flowed into the workforce, followed by a steady drop-off to 62 percent in 2022. With the current labor force at around 164 million workers, a 5 percent decline represents about 8 million jobs. That is a large number of missing workers.

Part of this decline reflects the aging of the U.S. labor force: The leading edge of the baby-boom generation has reached retirement age over the last decade. In addition, and mostly unrelated, the labor force participation rate among men has fallen from 88 percent in 1950 to 70 percent today, which mostly accounts for the overall drop in the participation rate.

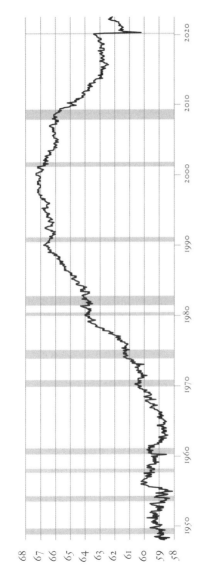

Figure 4: Labor Force Participation Rate, 1948–2020

Shaded areas indicate U.S. recessions

Source: U.S. Bureau of Labor Statistics, Labor Force Participation Rate [CIVPART], retrieved from FRED, Federal Reserve Bank of St. Louis; https://fred.stlouisfed.org/series/CIVPART, July 26, 2022.

As men represent about 54 percent of the labor force, a decline of 18 percent is the equivalent of about 15 million jobs in 2022.

On the other hand, labor force participation for women increased from 35 percent in the 1950s to 60 percent by the late 1990s, partly neutralizing the fall-off among men. The increased participation among women in that era undoubtedly boosted the overall growth rate from the 1960s through the 1990s compared to what it otherwise might have been. Female participation has declined slightly in recent years to 58 percent, so that this element in American economic growth appears to have run its course.

IV. PRODUCTIVITY

The other main element in economic growth (besides population) is the productivity of the labor force, generally defined as the ratio of Gross Domestic Product to hours worked. The labor force can remain stable or decline in size, but the economy can still grow if workers are more productive because they have more skills or because the capital at their disposal is more efficient, or both. Falling rates of productivity, mixed with a slowly growing workforce, are causes of slowing growth in the overall economy.

This appears to be what has happened in the United States across the post-war decades, but especially over the last twenty or so years. The advance of the computer age has not yet brought about the revolution in productivity that some technology experts predicted in the 1960s and 1970s. As the economist Robert Solow put it in the late 1980s, "the computer age is evident everywhere but in the productivity statistics."

The chart below illustrates percentage changes in labor force productivity from 1950 to 2021, again portrayed as five-year moving averages to highlight the overall trend and to smooth out fluctuations due to recessions and recoveries. Productivity growth surged to 4.5 percent per year in the mid-1960s at a time when the labor force was also expanding. These two developments in combination produced the robust economic growth of the 1960s.

But, contrary to expectations, productivity growth declined steadily through the 1970s while the number of workers surged with the entry of women and the baby-boom generation into the labor force. Productivity growth surged again briefly to over 3.5 percent per year in the late 1990s and early 2000s as businesses began to operate more efficiently with the introduction of new information technologies (personal computers and the internet). All told, the long-term rate of productivity growth from 1950 to 2000 was around 2.5 percent per year, with some significant fluctuations around that figure.

Yet, for reasons not well understood by economists, the surge in productivity that began in the 1990s was brief, lasting only until 2003 when those gains vanished as productivity spiraled downward to less than 1 percent per year in the decade following the financial crisis of 2007–08 – or less than half the long-term rate of 2.5 percent per year between 1950

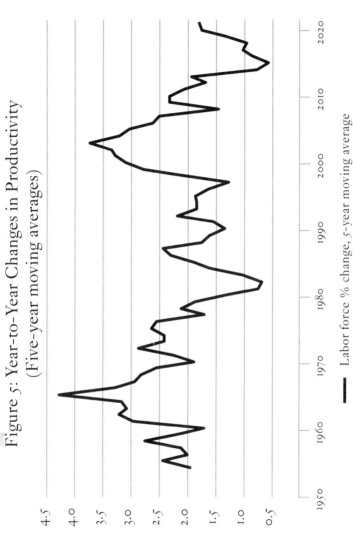

Figure 5: Year-to-Year Changes in Productivity (Five-year moving averages)

Labor force % change, 5-year moving average

Source: U.S. Bureau of Labor Statistics, Nonfarm Business Sector: Labor Productivity (Output per Hour) for All Employed Persons [OPHNFB], retrieved from FRED, Federal Reserve Bank of St. Louis; https://fred.stlouisfed.org/series/OPHNFB, July 26, 2022.

and 2000. That is another significant factor behind the economic slowdown of the past few decades.

There are signs in the past few years that productivity may be improving due to the introduction of digital technology: e-commerce, cloud computing, artificial intelligence and the like. Productivity grew by 2.5 percent in 2020 and nearly 2 percent in 2021, well above the anemic rate of previous years, though that may have been a function of the crash and recovery due to the pandemic. Yet there have been such signs in the past that dissipated before yielding long-term gains in worker productivity. It could easily happen again. On that point, productivity declined by 0.6 percent in the first quarter of 2022.

V. Debt as Substitute for Growth

Americans have responded in a logical way to slowing economic growth combined with historically low interest rates: They have borrowed and gone into debt to sustain their

Prior to the coronavirus pandemic, per capita income growth was running at just 1 or 2 percent per year, or roughly half the rate of the period from 1960 to 2000.

standard of living. They are hardly alone: Households, corporations and governments around the world have done much the same thing. Those decisions have created an unprecedented mountain of debt around the world and especially in the United States. As growth has slowed, debt has surged at every level.

Total credit market debt (government debt plus consumer and household debt plus corporate debt) in the world economy increased to $300 trillion by the end of 2021 against a world GDP of $100 trillion, or a ratio of 3 to 1. The situation is somewhat more alarming in the United States. The Federal Reserve Bank of St. Louis (see the chart below) calculates that total credit market debt in the U.S. is more than $90 trillion in 2022 as against a GDP of $23 trillion: a ratio of close to 4 to 1, and continuing to rise.

Debt has been growing here and abroad for more than three decades as a consequence of historically low interest rates, along with financial innovations that make debt far easier to issue and carry. From 1950 to 1980, the ratio of credit market debt to GDP in the United States hovered around 1.5 to 1, as shown in the chart below. After that time, the ratio steadily increased to 2.4 to 1 in 1990, 2.9 to 1 in 2000, 3.7 to 1 in 2010, and 4 to 1 today. Over that period, from 1980 to the present, total credit market debt increased by 20-fold compared to an eight-fold expansion in nominal GDP.

Many rightly focus on the size of the federal debt ($30.4 trillion currently) because it represents one-third of all outstanding debt while interest payments represent a rising share of federal expenditures. Gross federal debt has tripled from $10 to $30 trillion since

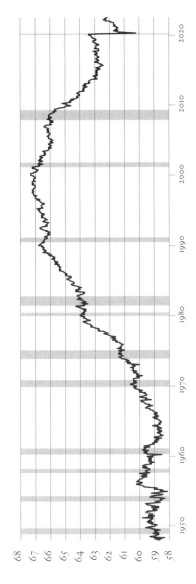

Figure 6: Total Credit Market Debt in United States, 1950–2021

Shaded areas indicate U.S. recessions

Source: Board of Governors of the Federal Reserve System (US), All Sectors; Debt Securities and Loans; Liability, Level [TCMDO], retrieved from FRED, Federal Reserve Bank of St. Louis; https://fred.stlouisfed.org/series/TCMDO, July 26, 2022.

the 2008 financial crisis, and (nearly) doubled in relation to GDP from 67 percent in 2008 to 123 percent today. The U.S. government spent $400 billion in net interest payments in 2021, roughly 6 percent of total federal expenditures of $6.8 trillion, though the budget was heavily inflated that year due to short-term spending on the coronivirus pandemic. In 2022 interest payments will consume more than 8 percent of federal spending, and possibly more if interest rates continue to increase.

Since 2001, the average annual interest rate on U.S. debt fell from 6.6 to 2 percent per year, substantially easing the debt burden but encouraging more of it. A return to "normal" rates of 6 or 7 percent would double or triple annual interest payments to the point where they crowd out other expenditures. The Congressional Budget Office, wary of rising interest rates, projects that federal spending on interest payments will exceed $1 trillion within ten years and will eventually surpass Medicare, Social Security and National Defense as the largest item in the federal budget.

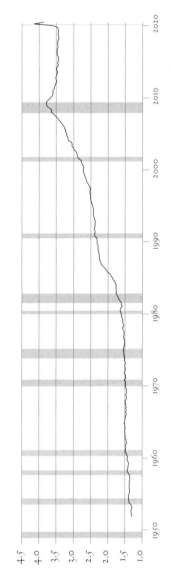

Figure 7: Total Credit Market Debt as Percentage of GDP

Shaded areas indicate U.S. recessions

Source: Board of Governors of the Federal Reserve System (US), All Sectors; Debt Securities and Loans; Liability, Level [TCMDO], retrieved from FRED, Federal Reserve Bank of St. Louis; https://fred.stlouisfed.org/graph/?g=WRM#, July 26, 2022.

Still, the federal debt represents a third of the total debt outstanding, with state and local governments ($3.3 trillion, not including pension obligations), corporations ($12.1 trillion), household and not-for profit debt ($4.5 trillion), mortgages ($15.7 trillion) and financial institutions ($18.5 trillion) making up most of the rest. Household debt, including mortgages, add up to 80 percent of GDP today. Corporations, also taking advantage of low real interest rates, doubled their borrowings in recent years from a total of $6 trillion in 2010 to more than $12.1 trillion in 2021, which also makes those organizations vulnerable to rising interest rates.

As the workforce expands more slowly, or as productivity slows, the overall economy will contract or expand more slowly as well.

These rising debt burdens here and elsewhere are linked to historically low interest rates but also to slowing economic growth and stagnating salaries and wages, such that incomes for households and institutions are more and more propped up by debt and government transfers of various kinds. This pattern has developed and accelerated over the past few decades as rates have fallen along with economic growth, and it could continue for some years to come – unless rising interest rates cause consumers, businesses and governments to scale back borrowing.

That appears to be happening as the prime rate of interest offered by banks has increased recently from 3.25 to 4.75 percent per year and is undoubtedly headed higher, to 6 percent or more. Those interest rates are far from unusual: During the 1990s, the prime rate ranged between 6 and 10 percent, yet the economy continued to grow at more than 3 percent per year. In any case, economists agree that debt at current levels will operate as a drag on future growth, and higher interest charges will add to the problem as the costs of servicing debt crowd out other household and institutional expenditures. For corporations, debts and debt service will crowd out funds otherwise available for capital goods, undermining productivity and reducing overall output. Those charges will reduce household consumption, an additional burden on future growth.

Some believe that rising interest rates may bring an end to a prolonged era of debt-financed consumption and a long and record-setting bull market in stocks and bonds. That may be so, but interest rates rise and fall for many reasons, including prospects for future growth along with responses by the Federal Reserve to rising prices. In recent years, rising rates, with current levels of debt, have caused the economy to stall, leading in turn to declines in interest rates in a continuing cycle of "go and stop." The underlying problem is that the economy, weighted down by debt, cannot find its footing to sustain an expansion.

VI. REMEDIES?

Is the American economy in secular decline? The answer is "yes." Is the growth deficit something Americans should be worried about? The answer, again, is "yes." Growth is gradually slowing across the economy, and has been for decades. The civilian labor force is now growing more slowly than in past decades when growth was more robust. Labor force productivity is similarly declining, though there may be possibilities for reversal there. Americans, like others around the world, have taken advantage of low interest rates to support their incomes with increasing debt. That debt, in turn, will act as a drag on future growth, particularly as interest rates rise.

Prominent economists have pointed to various factors behind slowing growth. The United States faces greater international competition today, which was not the case in the early post-war years when nearly all competitors were recovering from war. Manufacturing has given way to services, where it is more difficult to squeeze out productivity gains. Companies continue to outsource manufacturing to foreign countries. New technologies do not promote economic growth and productivity as much as former breakthroughs in electricity, the internal combustion engine, fossil fuels and low-cost energy and other innovations of the 19th and 20th centuries.

There are other headwinds, as Robert Gordon calls them in *The Rise and Fall of American Growth*. Educational attainment is slowing. The labor force is not expanding as in the past. The population is aging. Americans are heavily in debt. Income inequality is reducing consumption. Efforts to deal with climate change will increase energy costs across the economy. Those are formidable obstacles to growth.

Professor Gordon and others have cautiously suggested various remedies to reverse the downward trends. These include: levying higher taxes on the wealthy, raising the minimum wage, spending more on education (especially pre-school programs), revising immigration policies that bring in skilled workers, revising patent and licensing regulations to encourage innovation, eliminating regressive zoning regulations that raise housing costs and impede mobility in urban areas, and addressing the federal government's addiction to debt through tax and spending reforms.

Some of these ideas may prove helpful, such as reforms in patents, licensing, zoning and immigration policies, which could win broad support. But they would be band-aids that will do little to address the larger challenges of growth. Other ideas are unlikely to

---

Over the past two decades the workforce expanded by less than half the rate of the 1980s, and by less than a third of the rate during the 1970s.

---

yield positive results and may further undermine economic growth. The minimum wage, for example, has been increased regularly since the 1950s without doing anything to promote employment or growth. It may have opposite effects, as many economists say. Spending on education has increased steadily over the years while student achievement has declined at a roughly similar rate. Spending more money on union-controlled schools is unlikely to do anything to promote student achievement or long-run productivity.

Taxing the rich is an idea long favored by Democrats, though it would not do much to reduce inequality because those funds would flow into the federal government to be disbursed in turn to government employees and well-positioned interest groups. Besides, much of that wealth is earned in the form of capital gains, which are taxed at lower rates than salaries and wages. Increases in those taxes would discourage risk, investment and innovation, which is not what anyone wants. Finally, bringing the federal budget under control and into balance would be a great help, but it will take heroic efforts by the parties, or probably a crisis of some kind, to bring it about. The parties in charge have balanced the budget exactly once since 1970.

Behind these discrete proposals lies a larger and probably intractable problem: The American economy is gradually being squeezed by the growth of government and the interest groups that are attached to it. The U.S. economy grew rapidly from 1870 to 1940, as Professor Gordon writes, because of the introduction of new technologies and consumer products, but also because political headwinds in the form of large governments and well-positioned interest groups were not yet in place to block them. During those decades the federal government did not do much besides run a post office and some custom houses and maintain a modest law enforcement apparatus, while spending (except in war time) about 2 percent of GDP.

The most influential lobbies at that time were mostly industry groups of one kind or another.

The situation is far different today. Over the past century, since the Great Depression and the New Deal followed by the reforms of the Great Society and many others in subsequent decades, the federal government has assumed a supervisory role in relation to the economy through regulations on business and policies that favor investment or disinvestment in various sectors – domestic energy producers being prime examples of the latter. The reforms of the 1960s led to new groups and regulatory institutions demanding further supervision of business in the name of consumer protection, worker safety, the environment, civil rights and many other causes. The Democratic Party, a pro-growth institution through most of the 20th century, is now consumed by other themes, especially race and gender ideology, public employee unions and climate change. It is not necessarily "anti-growth," but growth is no longer at the center of its deliberations. It may require two sympathetic parties and a generally favorable political environment to promote the kind of growth the United States enjoyed through much of the last century. Such a political climate, once characteristic of the United States, is no longer in place. It is hard to know how to bring it back.

The late Mancur Olson argued in *The Rise and Decline of Nations* (1982) that it is difficult to sustain economic growth in stable polities because it will be undermined over time by the formation of interest groups focused more on the distribution of resources than in their production. The formation of these groups, along with the influence they wield within governments, impedes an economy's ability to adopt innovative technologies and reallocate resources to new areas as conditions change and opportunities arise. Prosperity leads to cartels, unions, pressure groups and lobbies of various kinds that gradually take over governments and turn them into barriers to further growth. They infiltrate and take over political parties, or form new ones, as they advance their causes. Those groups promote new regulatory bodies, encourage complexity and uncertainty in regulation and cause a general enlargement of the role of government in relation to business and the economy. They raise prices, seek control over investment and disinvestment and generally sow confusion in society about the obstacles

Americans have responded in a logical way to slowing economic growth combined with historically low interest rates: They have borrowed and gone into debt to sustain their standard of living.

to growth and the operations of business and government. Governments afflicted by these conditions usually require traumatic shocks to dissolve them, such as wars, revolutions and depressions. Olson observed how the Revolution, Civil War and the Great Depression applied such shocks to the American system, and how wars have done so in other countries, Germany and Japan in the post-war decades serving as prime examples. Those events, notwithstanding the damage they caused, led to constructive economic outcomes.

This is a good description of what has happened in the United States in recent decades as government has become more active in all areas while growth in the economy has gradually stalled. No one wants to see a traumatic "shock" to dissolve the system, but the policy proposals advanced by economists, such as more spending on education or raising the minimum wage, will not be up to the task of changing the overall political environment in the direction of growth and prosperity. The growth deficit is a large and long-running development; it may require a sequence of equally impressive events, such as a depression, financial crisis or political upheaval, to reverse it. The alternative may be many years of continuing economic stagnation along with simmering political unrest as incomes and future prospects stagnate as well. If there were an easy way out, then we would not have gotten into this situation in the first place.

First American edition published in 2022 by Encounter Books,
an activity of Encounter for Culture and Education, Inc.,
a nonprofit, tax-exempt corporation.
Encounter Books website address: www.encounterbooks.com

Manufactured in the United States and printed on
acid-free paper. The paper used in this publication meets
the minimum requirements of ANSI / NISO z39.48–1992
(R 1997) (*Permanence of Paper*).

A portion of this Broadside pamphlet appeared in
the *Wall Street Journal* on July 15, 2022, and has been
reproduced with permission from the publication.

FIRST AMERICAN EDITION

LIBRARY OF CONGRESS CATALOGING-IN-PUBLICATION DATA
IS AVAILABLE